I0462191

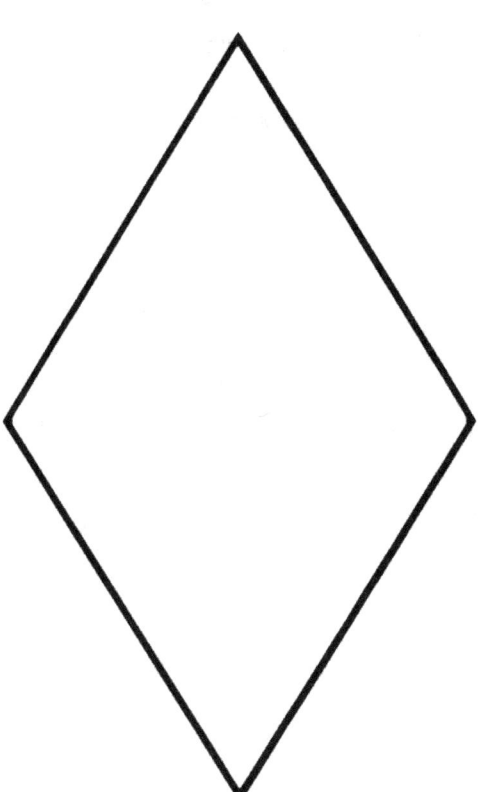

< Other titles by Nanos Valaoritis
with drawing(s) by Marie Wilson >

La boîte de Pandore, L'Harmattan, Paris, 2008

Flash Bloom, Wire Press, San Francisco, 1980

Central Arcade, privately published, Athens, 1958

Terre de diamant, privately published, Athens, 1958

< Artist's Monograph >

Daedalic Isomorphs of Marie Wilson, Hellenic American Union,
Athens, 2000

< Other titles by Nanos Valaoritis in English >

Pan Daimonium, Philos Press, Lacey, 2005

My Afterlife Guaranteed, City Lights, San Francisco, 1990

Diplomatic Relations, Panjandrum, San Francisco, 1972

Hired Hieroglyphs, Kayak Books, Santa Clara, 1971

< Also from *Rêve à Deux* >

Sotère Torregian *Surreal Adventurer,* 2015

Sotère Torregian *The Age of Gold (Redux)*, 2014

Will Alexander *The Brimstone Boat – For Philip Lamantia*, 2012

Schlechter Duvall *The Adventures of Desirée,* 2009

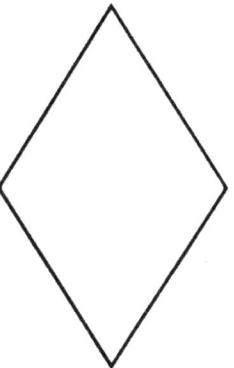

Land of Diamond

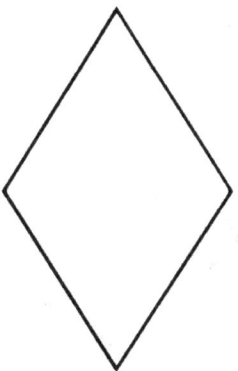

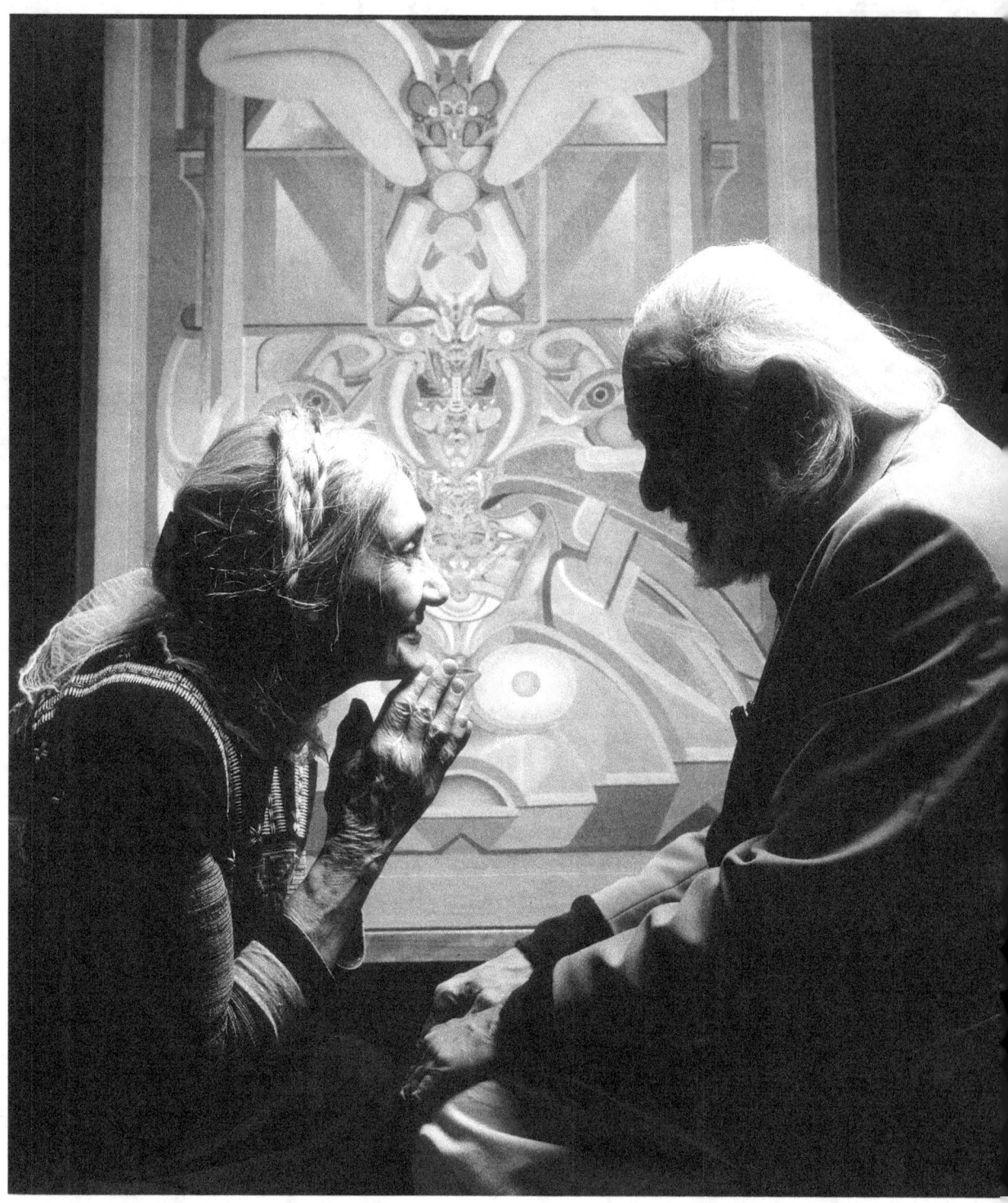

Marie and Nanos, Athens, 2000   Photograph by Tassos Vrettos

Land of Diamond

Sixteen Drawings by MARIE WILSON

Parallel Texts by NANOS VALAORITIS

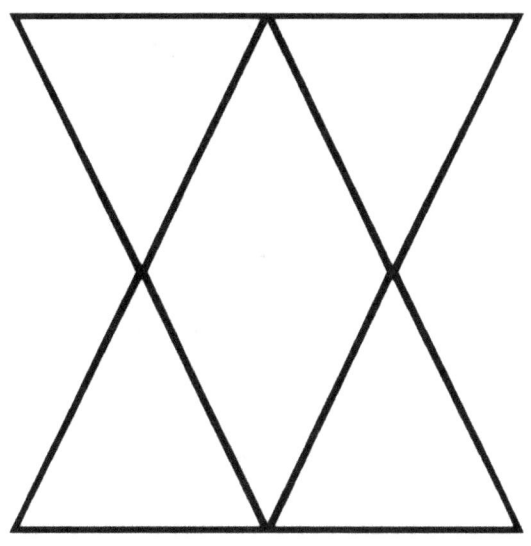

Rêve à Deux

Oakland - Athens - Vacaville

Copyright © 2015 by Marie Wilson

The cover design is by Thom Burns.

Cover Image, "Vehicle of the Gods," 1958 © by Marie Wilson;
back cover photograph (detail), and page 4, frontispiece
photograph, "Marie and Nanos, Athens, 2000" © by
Tassos Vrettos.

⋆

Editor's Notes:

The original sixteen drawings of *Terre de diamant* were
reproduced uniquely as lithographs. This edition derives from the
best examples of each lithograph which could be gleaned from
three copies of that book. The drawings appear here in a slightly
larger size than they did originally.

Nanos Valaoritis provided the English translation of the French text.

⋆

Rêve à Deux

Rêve à Deux would like to thank Tassos Vrettos for his permission
to use his photograph of Marie and Nanos for the frontispiece and
backcover of this book.

Rêve à Deux was founded in 2009, and is edited by Richard Waara.
Additional paperback copies of this book, and other
Rêve à Deux titles, are available on Amazon.com or Lulu.com.
Hardback editions of most of our titles are available
exclusively at: http://www.lulu.com

ISBN 978-0-578-16148-8 (Black & White Paperback Edition);
ISBN 978-0-578-16149-5 (Color Paperback Edition)

BLACK & WHITE PAPERBACK EDITION

Printed in the United States of America

To our friends

who inspired us, encouraged us, and helped us to realize this book,

Elisa and André Breton, Manina and Alain
Jouffroy, Charles Estienne, Jean Varda,
Wolfgang Paalen, Robert Benayoun, Philip
Sherrard, Nikos Gatsos, Georges Makris,
Jacques Lacarrière, Andreas Embirikos

I am the awakening voice in the eternal night. I begin now to deliver the controlling power of the veil of chaos. The power of the abysmal silt that brings and carries the mud of eternal and mute humidity; the whole power, always in movement, aqueous convulsions, which take that which is unmoving, holding what is tottering, freeing what comes, comforting that which rests, destroys what believes, the faithful guardian of the trace of the airs, she that derives joy from that which poured out on the order of the twelve eyes, that reveals the seal to the power that reigns in the middle of the invisible water, power that had been called the sea. This power, the ignorant called it Kronos; Kronos that had been chained when he had closed the net of Tartarus, thick and nebulous, obscure and dark.

PERATE GNOSTIQUE FRAGMENT

The Palace of the Eyes

The Palace of the Eyes

Two celestial bodies approach and hover like a gigantic dragonfly on the surface of the water, at an equal fragile and delicate distance of one another. They have been formed "by a widespread substance in the infinite, the great Telesma. Whenever it produces splendor it is called light. This light is the common mirror of all thoughts and forms, it holds the images of everything that has ever existed, the reflections of past worlds and by analogy the drafts of worlds to come."* It is the domain of the eyes, in its absolute multiplicity, where all is received, where nothing is lost, not even the shadow of a doubt. The polarization is perfect. Those who are observed by this miracle can feel again in themselves the release of a delicate mechanism, that causes all lived sensations, during a lifetime, even the most fleeting, to be registered, here, in the Palace of the Eyes. These omnivorous eyes, are capable of assimilating the most scattered things in their peacefulness and complexity, this retina of the world, this first reflection of the interior world.

*ELIPHAS LEVI: THE KEY OF THE GREAT MYSTERIES

< The Palace of the Eyes >

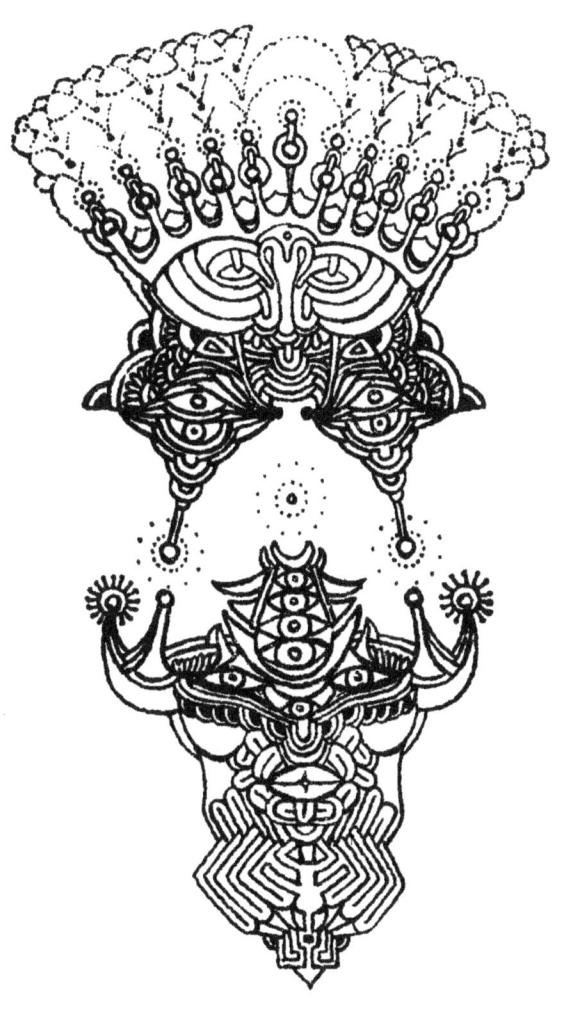

The Door of the Serpents

The Door of the Serpents

The Great Principle, to protect itself, projects high up disconcerting images and mirages. To suggest the strangeness of being, it creates one of these illusions that is the Door of the Serpents. Behind it, the way of the sun is opening, through the clouds of senses and of sexuality. It is the sumptuous shadow of absolute light.

< The Door of the Serpents >

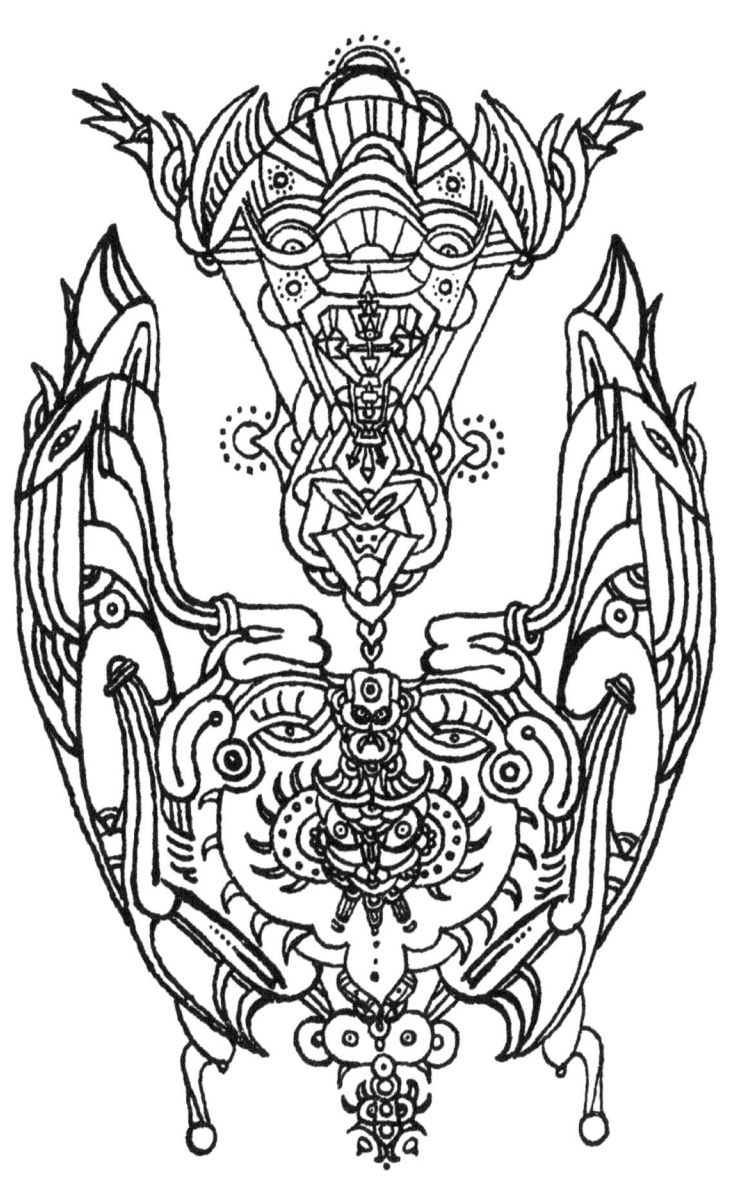

The Demon of the Sky

The Demon of the Sky

The Demon of the Sky is a metallic man: "His head is gold, which is the sun. Chest and arms of silver, which are the moon. The belly and thighs of copper which are Venus. The legs of iron which is Mars, and the feet half iron and clay that are violence and weakness. These four metallic parts correspond to the four ages of poets, to the four great periods of the historical universal cycle. This reign of gold founded on the iron and clay, namely, on the violence and weakness, has to be destroyed by the revelation of the cubic rock... that, detached from the mountain, will come to strike his feet of iron and clay and reduce him to dust."*

*ELIPHAS LEVI: THE KEY OF THE GREAT MYSTERIES

< The Demon of the Sky >

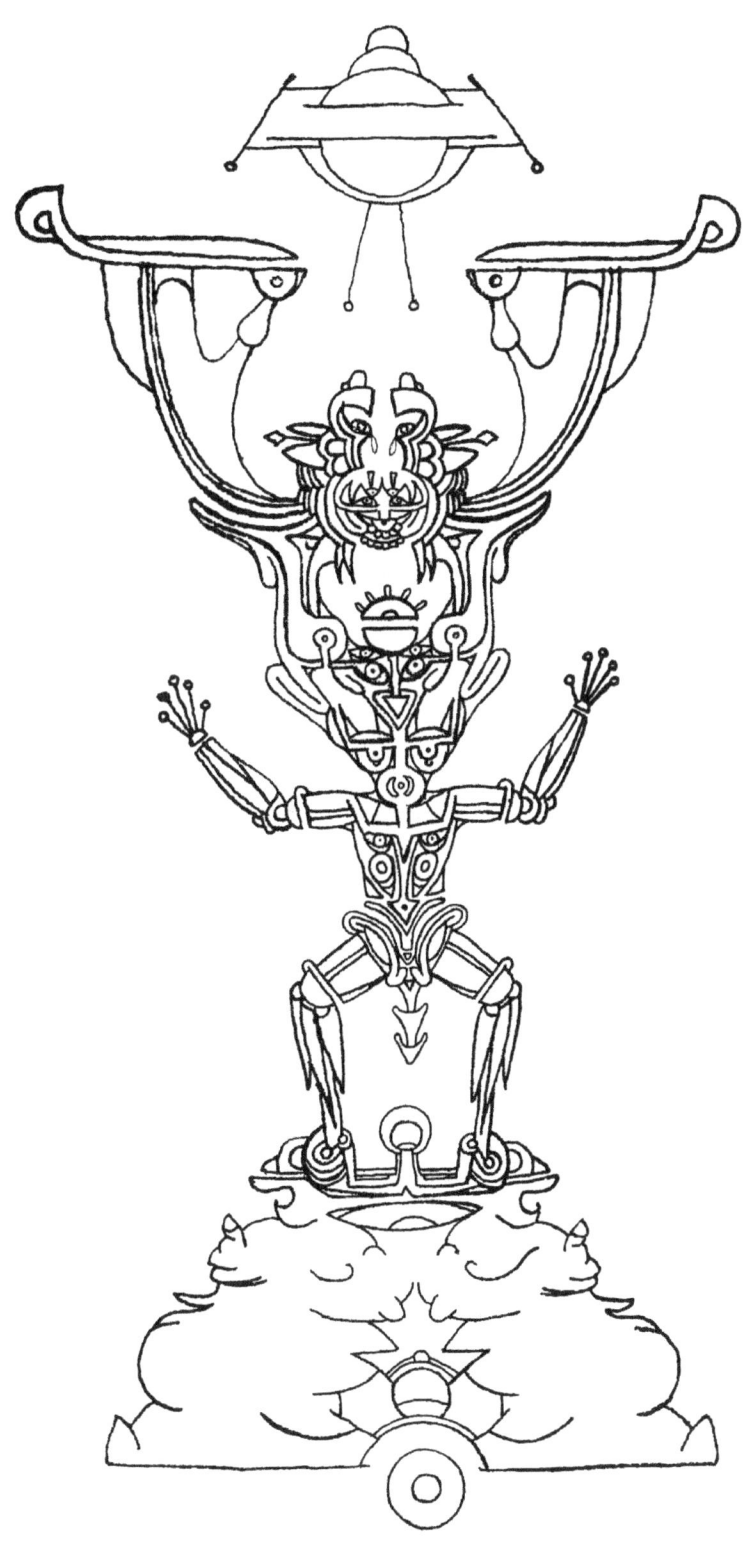

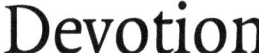

Devotion

Devotion

Naturally it is winged. Its wings like those of a scarab are hard and opaque close to the head, transparent depending on how they descend on its body. Armed from head to toe with the weapons that gave it the power over the soul, piloted by the flying eye with which it finds itself in permanent contact, its inferior part composing two claws that unite a planetary system. Its two arms are fixed in an attitude of hierarchical prayer, their extremities mingling together to form its mouth. Its flight is immobile, suspended in space; it is a presence that visits us in the hours of intense emotion before the marvelous being, before the prehistoric image, the exceptional stone of beauty, the flashing insect, the superior animal. It is the emblem of the very high Devotion.

< Devotion >

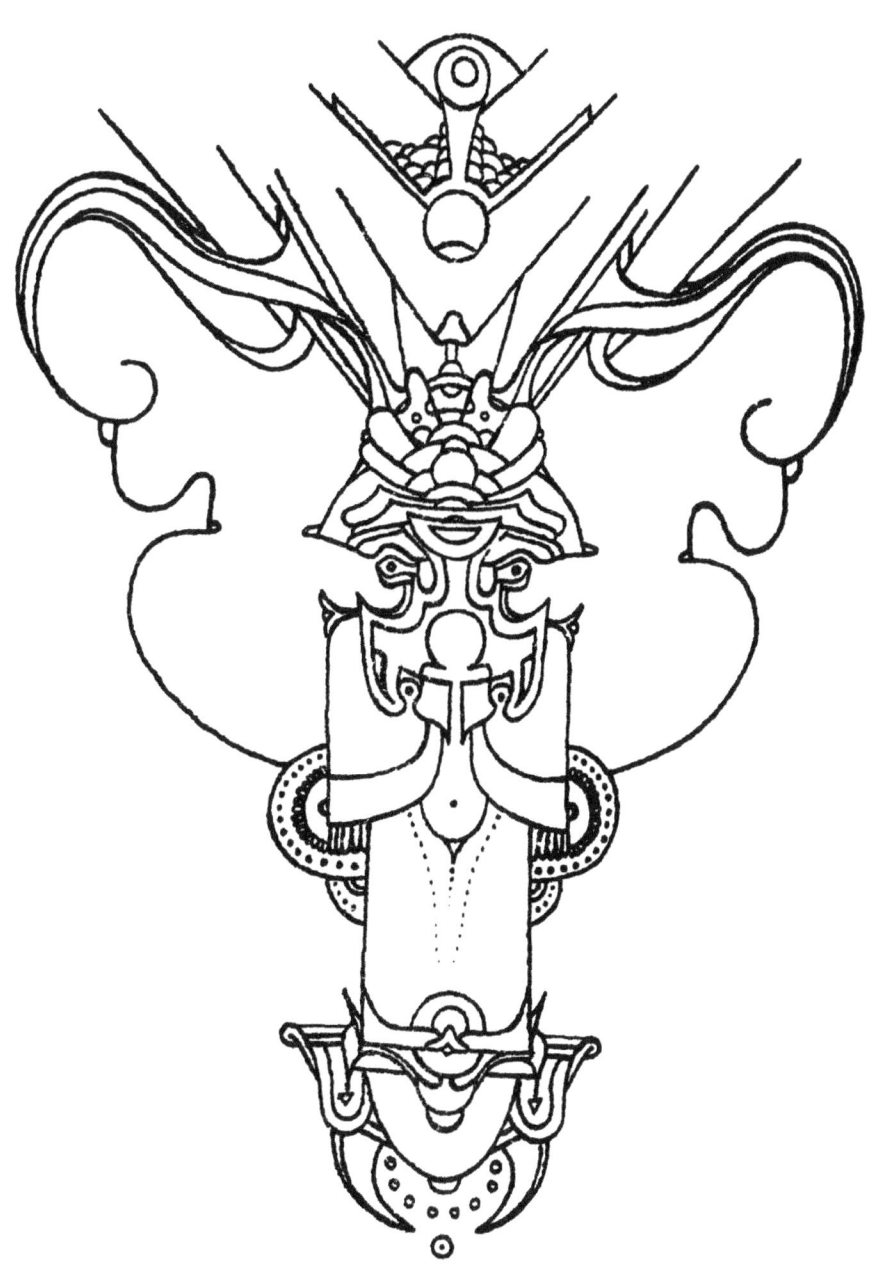

The Diamond Belt

The Diamond Belt

Situated in the middle of the exterior ocean, this arch of cut diamond according to the principles of a magic order, it contains in it the spirit of the equilibrium of the world. For those that have the eye sufficiently exercised, it constitutes in the profound night an enlightened and cosmic lighthouse, visible even from the other end of the universe, invisible though from close by as a dead star. It is impossible to attain, by ordinary means, for its exact position varies minute by minute. Founded on the black waters of the terrestrial moon, connected from the sun to nine planets, from an identical anti-sun and from Venus under its double aspect of the morning star and the evening star, the diamond stone carries on its summit the unchangeable heavenly body, from where emanates the green light that announces the end of the world.

< The Diamond Belt >

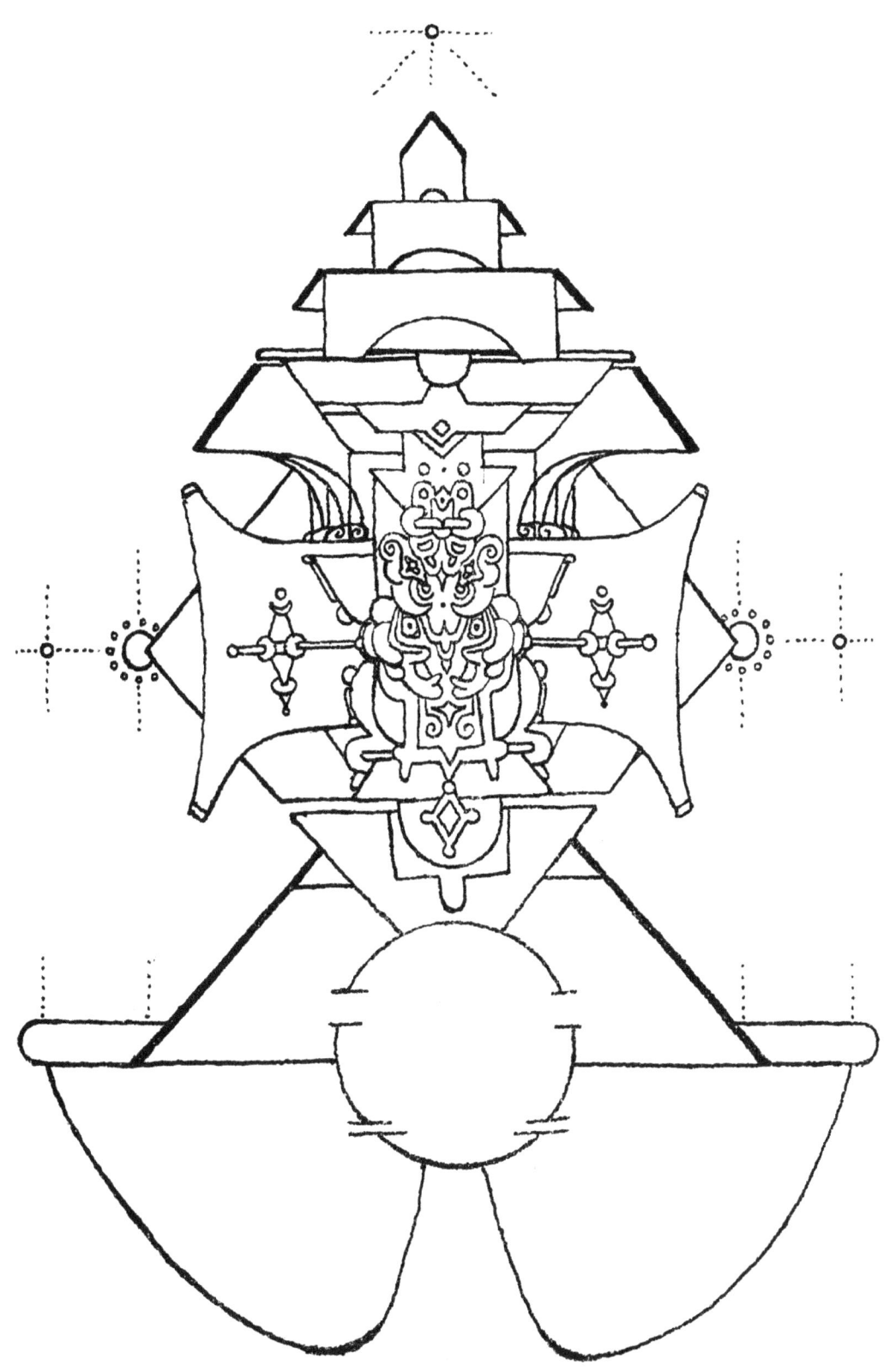

The Condition of The Slave

The Condition of The Slave

The spirit of the soul enslaved in the circle of the co-existence appears, tortured by hate and powerlessness. In it three animal spirits are stockpiled without leaving any letup, the desire of the solar plexus, the vaginal and abdominal desire. Apocalyptic image of despair and possession, incarnated by evil fairies and malevolent genies, she immobilizes in herself the reproductive sperm and semen. The interior daggers and blades, the brain full of teeth of hate and horror, the mutilated arms indicate self-destruction. She is the monstrous image of perpetual enslavement.

< The Condition of The Slave >

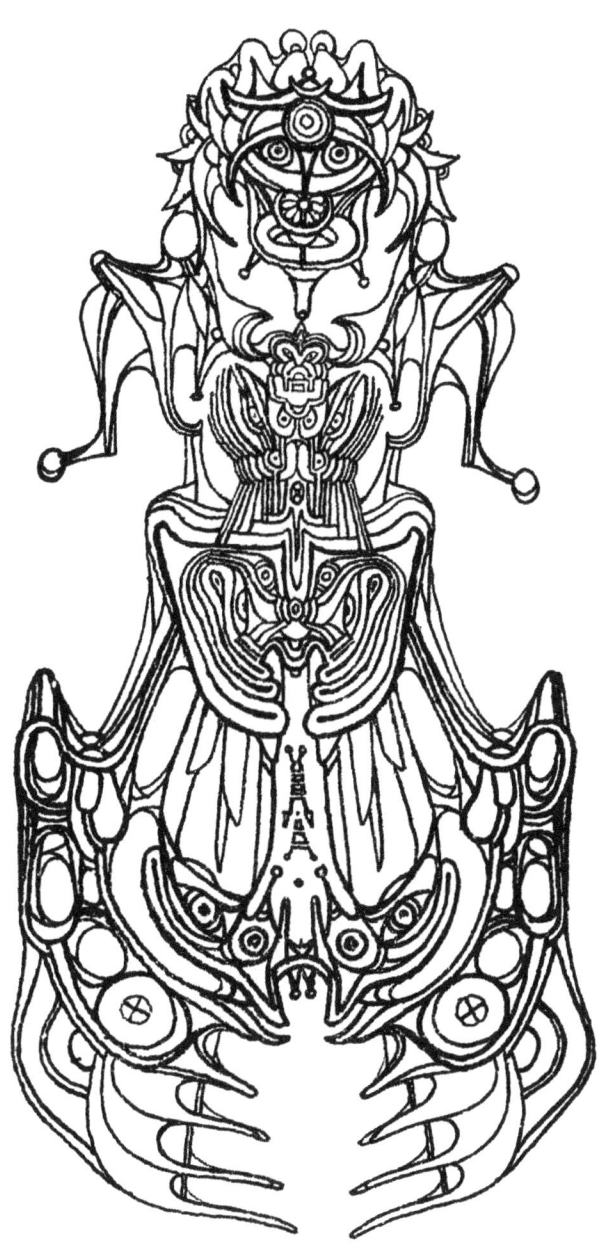

On the Threshold of Knowledge

On the Threshold of Knowledge

A pale blue light transmitted by the astral moon and its two Nordic quarters, reveals the Palace of Knowledge, bathed in the millennial calm and silence. It is the vision of a secret city, the apparition of which coincides with the beginning and the end of the cycle of history. The ten-thousand years, a period of accumulation of wisdom and preparation towards knowledge, are reflected by the central eye, surrounded by a labyrinth without entrance nor exit. The two auxiliary eyes on the sides receive in their urns the residue of thoughts scattered in the world. This place without guardian, will manifest itself, only at the beginning of the esoteric age, when the secret tradition will be revealed to the people, liberated at last from their enslavement to the Princes of Power and their avid desire for more.

< On the Threshold of Knowledge >

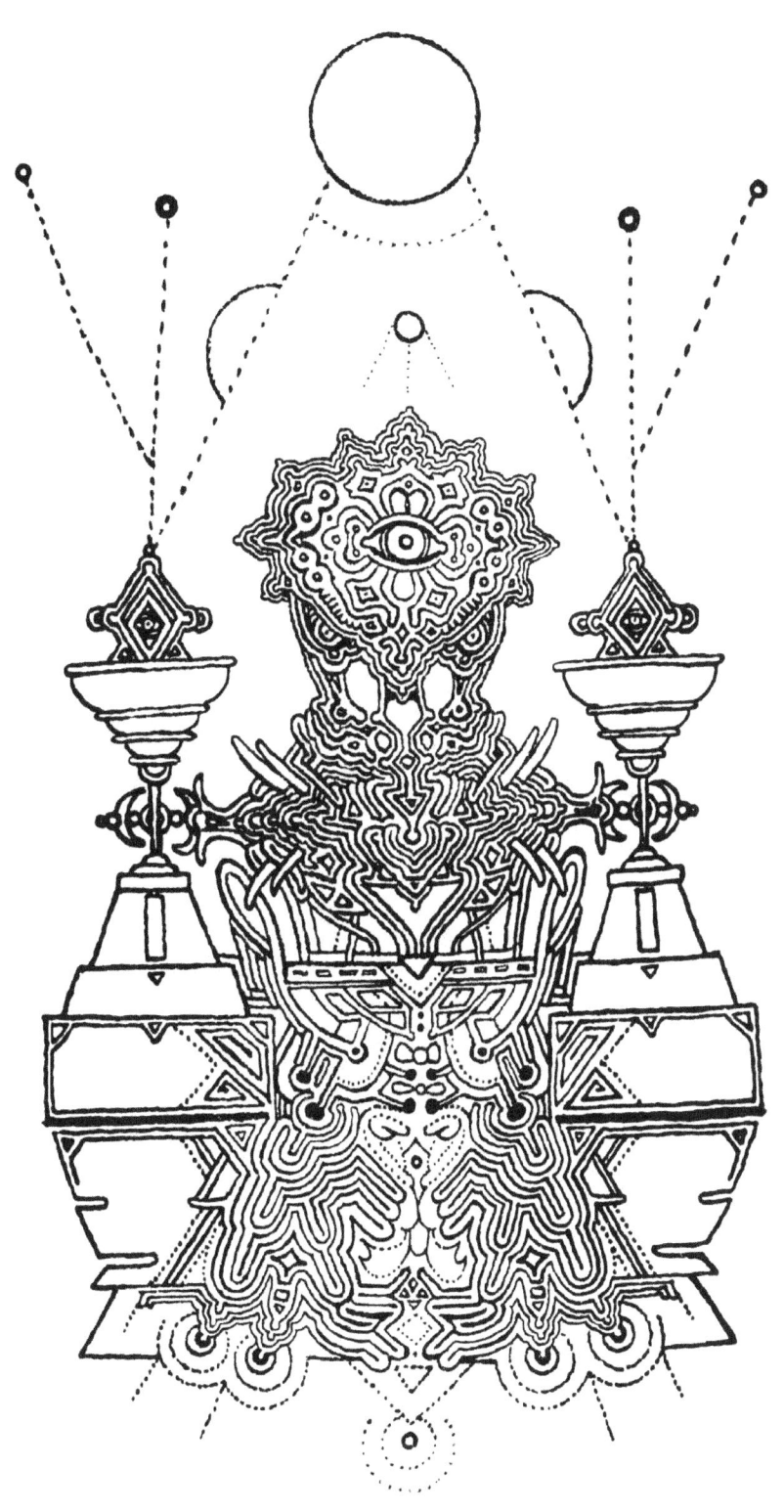

Apparition of the Spirit

Apparition of the Spirit

On its forehead are arrayed the eight towers of wisdom, surrounded by two minuscule suns. Towards the center where the mouth is located the six elements radiate: water, air, earth, and fire, time and space, similarly matching the six movements that, according to Plato, compose the universe. Visited and nourished by the cosmic bird, its feline nature reveals its mysterious and demonic essence, between man and animal, reality and dream, life and death. Its initiating horns contain the chaos; its apparition coincides with the moments of anger and illumination by violence. It is the guardian of the seventh door of the Terrestrial Paradise.

< Apparition of the Spirit >

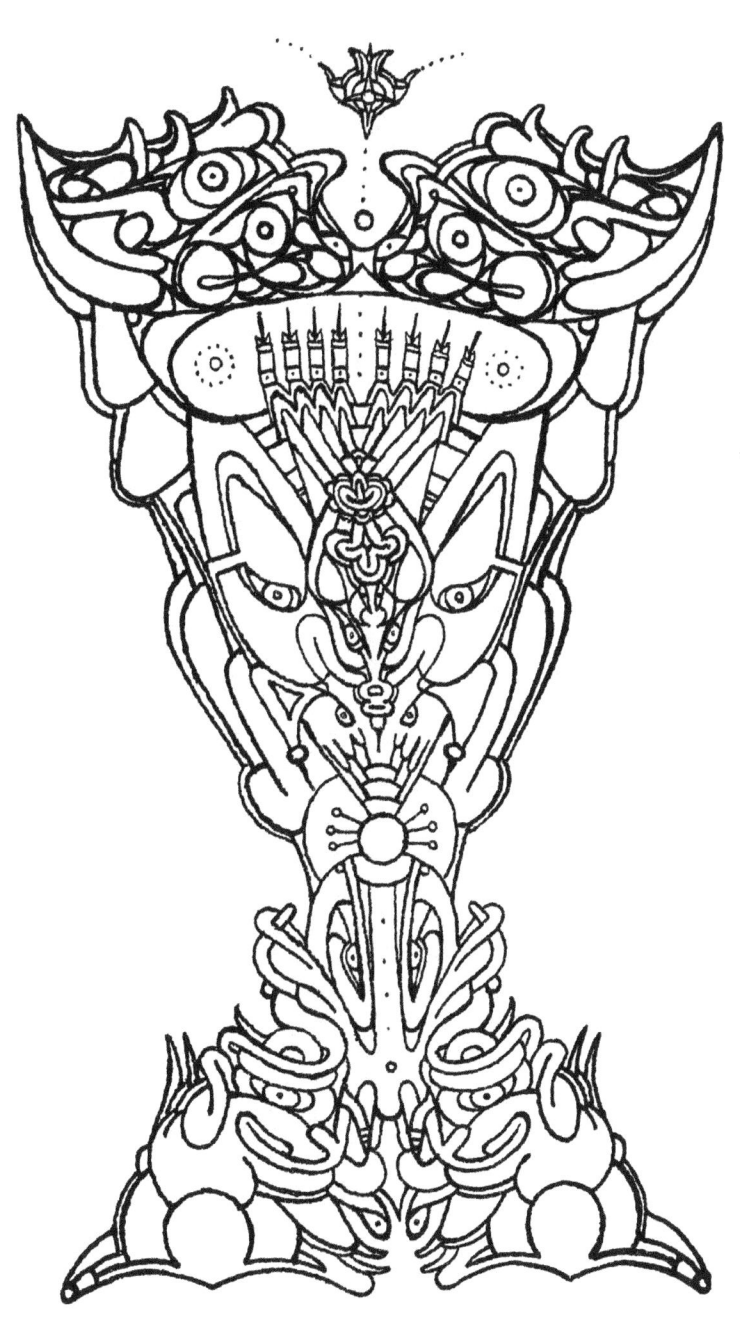

The Interior Sovereign

The Interior Sovereign

Guardian of the Egg that contains the Astral Body with its eleven satellites, its face is a mask of gold and its eyes are moonstones. It is entirely encrusted of opals, sapphires, and agates. At the edge of its head a stamen is assaulted by the pollen of the Milky Way. It fertilizes the women with the rays of a star, the grains of the trees, the water of rivers, and with a quick glance like the flight of a bird. It is the < master of the ceremonies that preside over the love of animals and plants >. It represents the glory and mystery of this world.

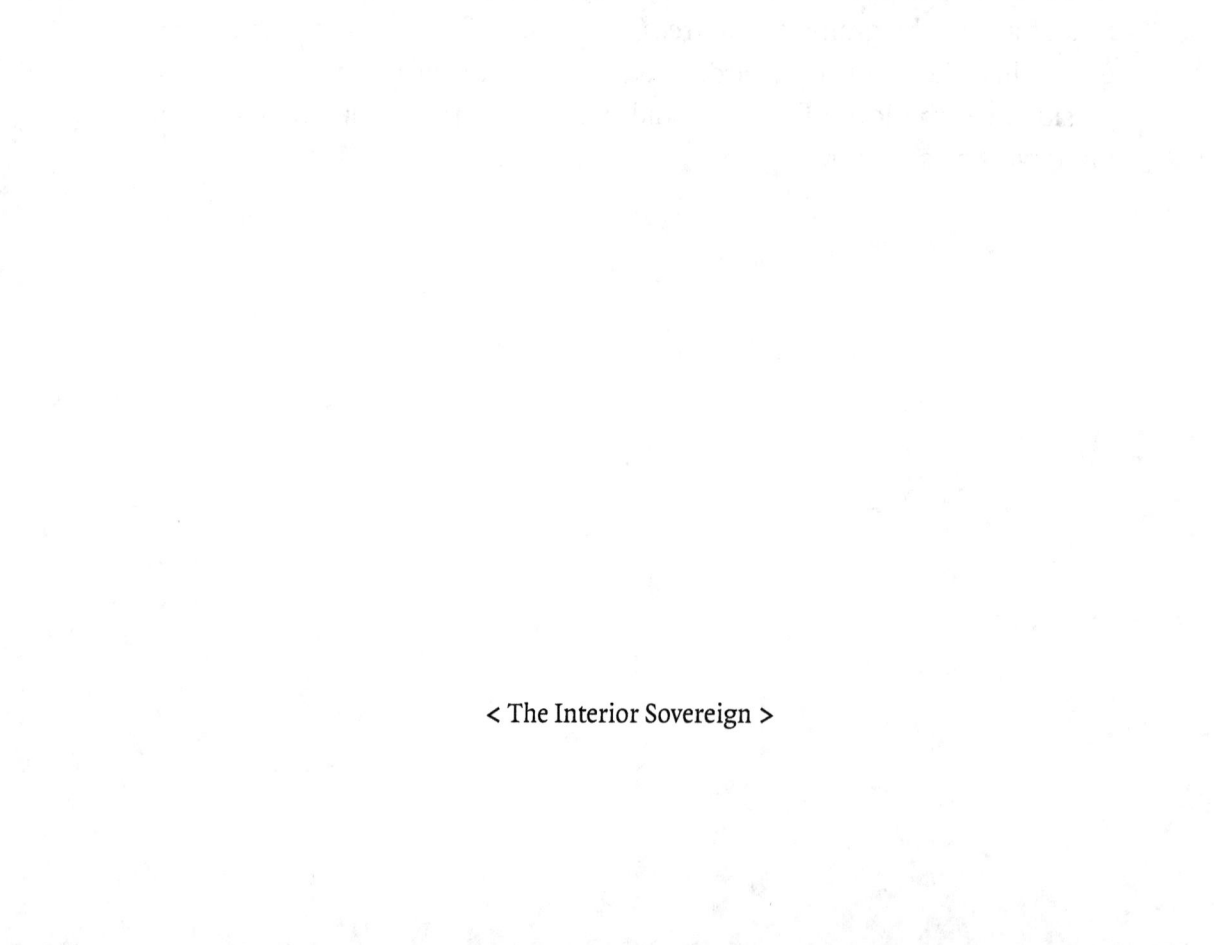

< The Interior Sovereign >

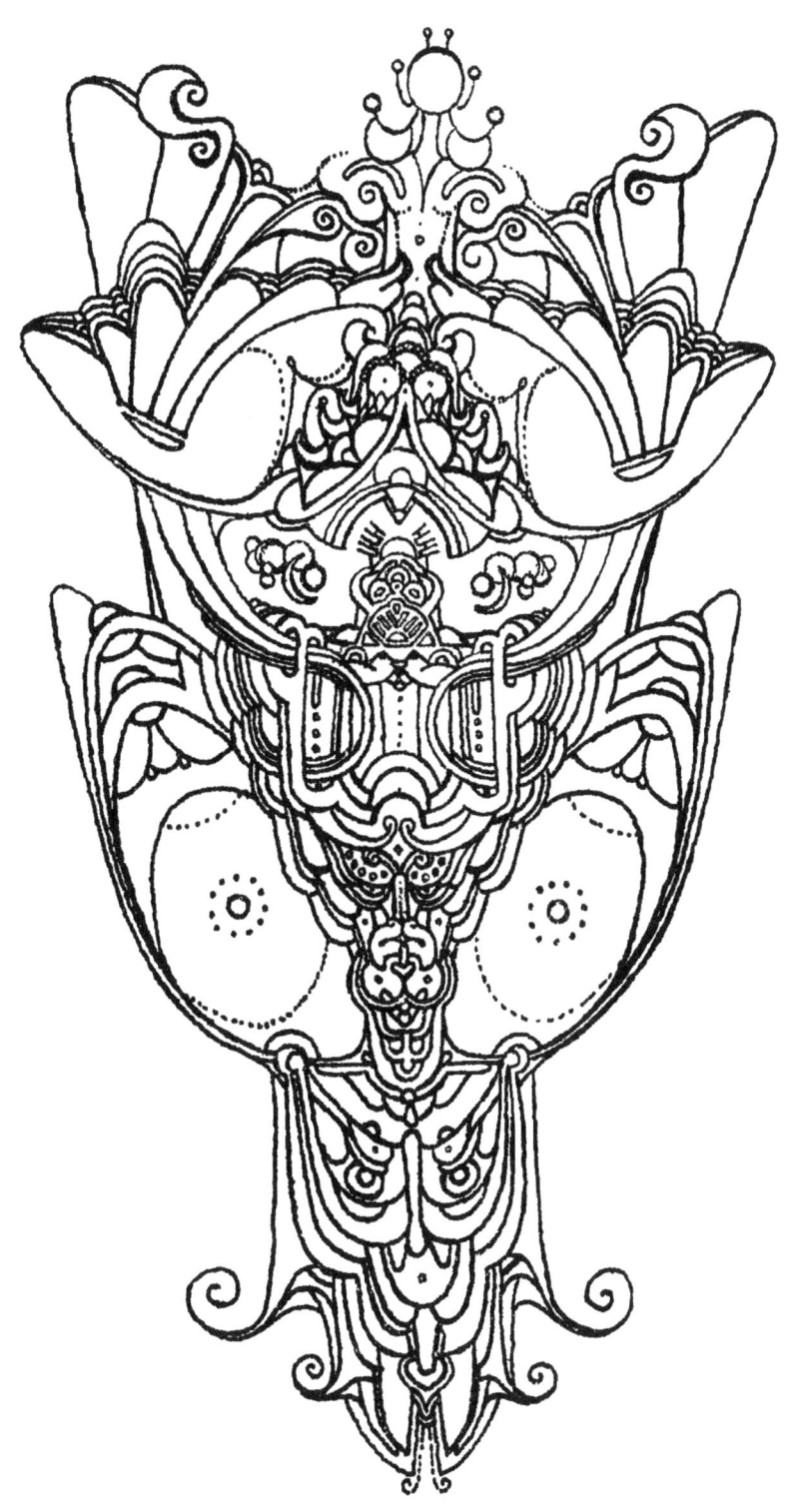

The Origin of the Universe

The Origin of the Universe

"He created time and the divisions of time, the constellations, the planets, the flowers, the seas, the mountains, the plains, the unequal ground.

"The austere devotion, voluptuousness, desire, anger, and this creation, for he wanted to give existence to all beings.

"He created the stars, the lightning, the clouds, the colored arches of Indra, the meteorites, the waterspouts, the comets, and the stars of diverse grandeur...

"The beasts, the savage beasts, the carnivorous animals deprived of a double row of teeth, the giants, the Vampires and the men, all of them born from one matrix.

"Surrounded by the quality of obscurity manifested under a multitude of forms, because of their preceding actions, these beings, endowed with an interior consciousness, feel keenly pleasure and pain.

"Such have been declared, from Brahma all the way to the vegetables, the transmigrations of this frightening world which endlessly destroys itself.

THE LAWS OF MANU, BOOK I

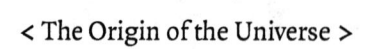
< The Origin of the Universe >

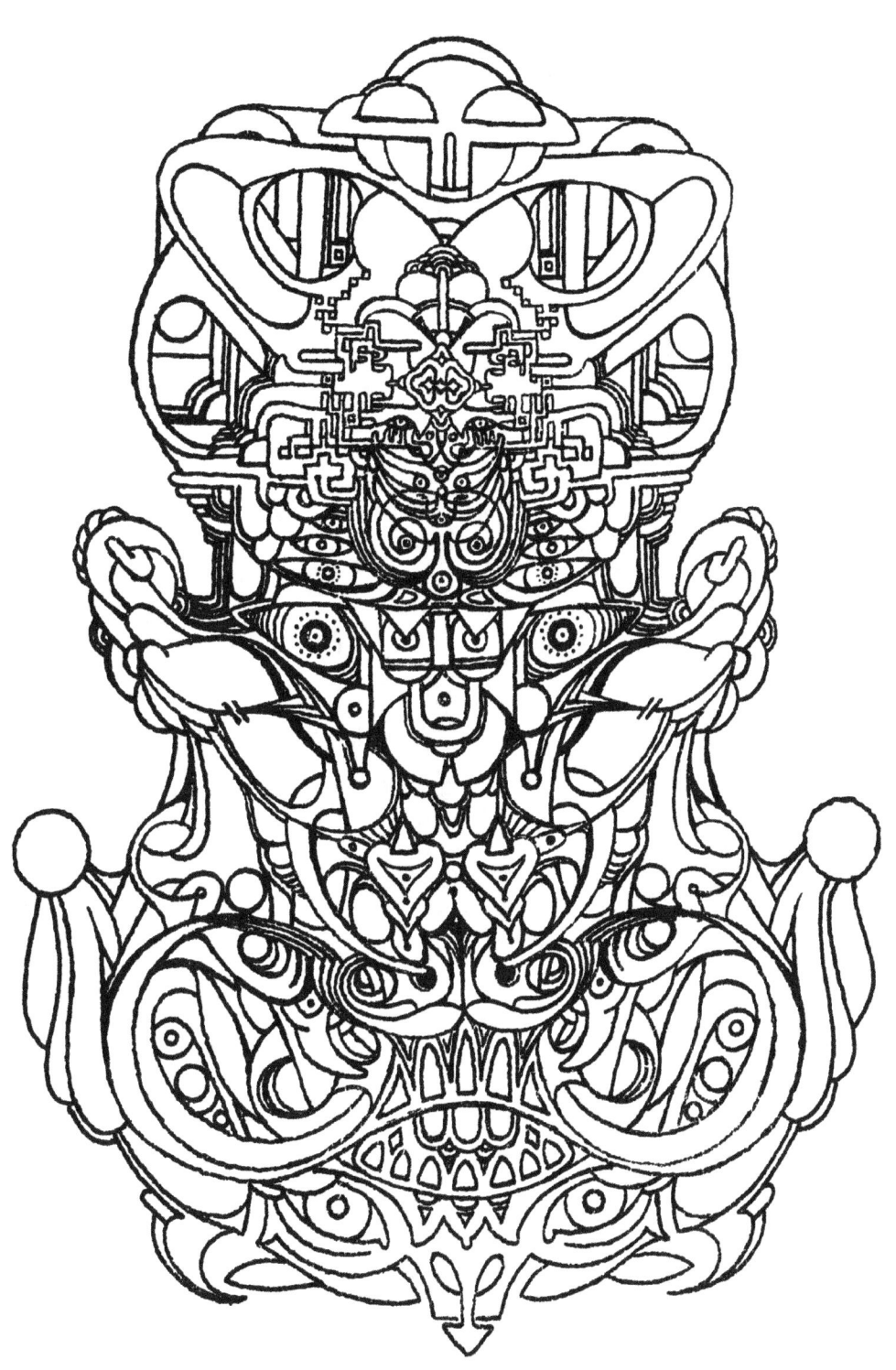

The Spirit of the Desert

The Spirit of the Desert

Overpopulated by dreams that occupy forcefully the isolated spirit, far from sources, from wells, and from rivers, it manifests itself also at the heart of the destroyed or abandoned cities, under the influence of drugs and fever. The mariners know it well; it visits the ships of the shipwrecked, dying of hunger and thirst; it creates the hallucinations and delirium at the confines of the visible and invisible. It is the Ram sacred to Zeus-Ammon with the sun between its horns, the oracle of the desert.

< The Spirit of the Desert >

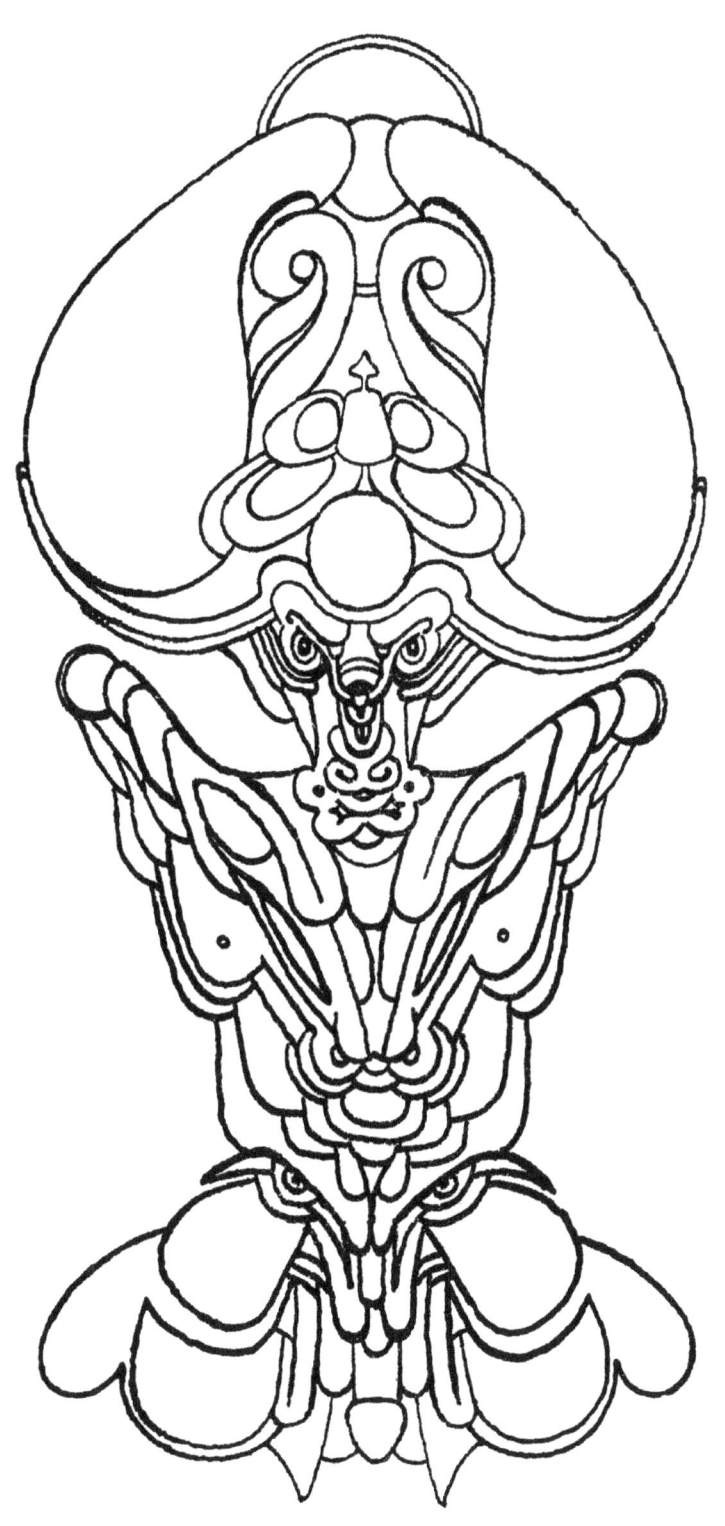

The Archangel of Pleasure

The Archangel of Pleasure

The Archangel of Pleasure falling from the sky, like lightning, crosses all beings. From the heart of the castle of Eblis, he eternally turns on his hinges creating the dizziness of ecstasy. From his sword spurts forth the spark of the desire for pleasure before the interdiction. It is he who created the virgins of Paradise, "still inviolate by the glance of men or of genies, the houris with beautiful black eyes, same as pearls in their mother of pearl."* It is he who created the Garden of Delights on the command of his Master, before the divinity was separated from pleasure, before the downfall of the angels and the reign of the warriors of Heaven or Hell, enemies of love.

*THE KORAN

< The Archangel of Pleasure >

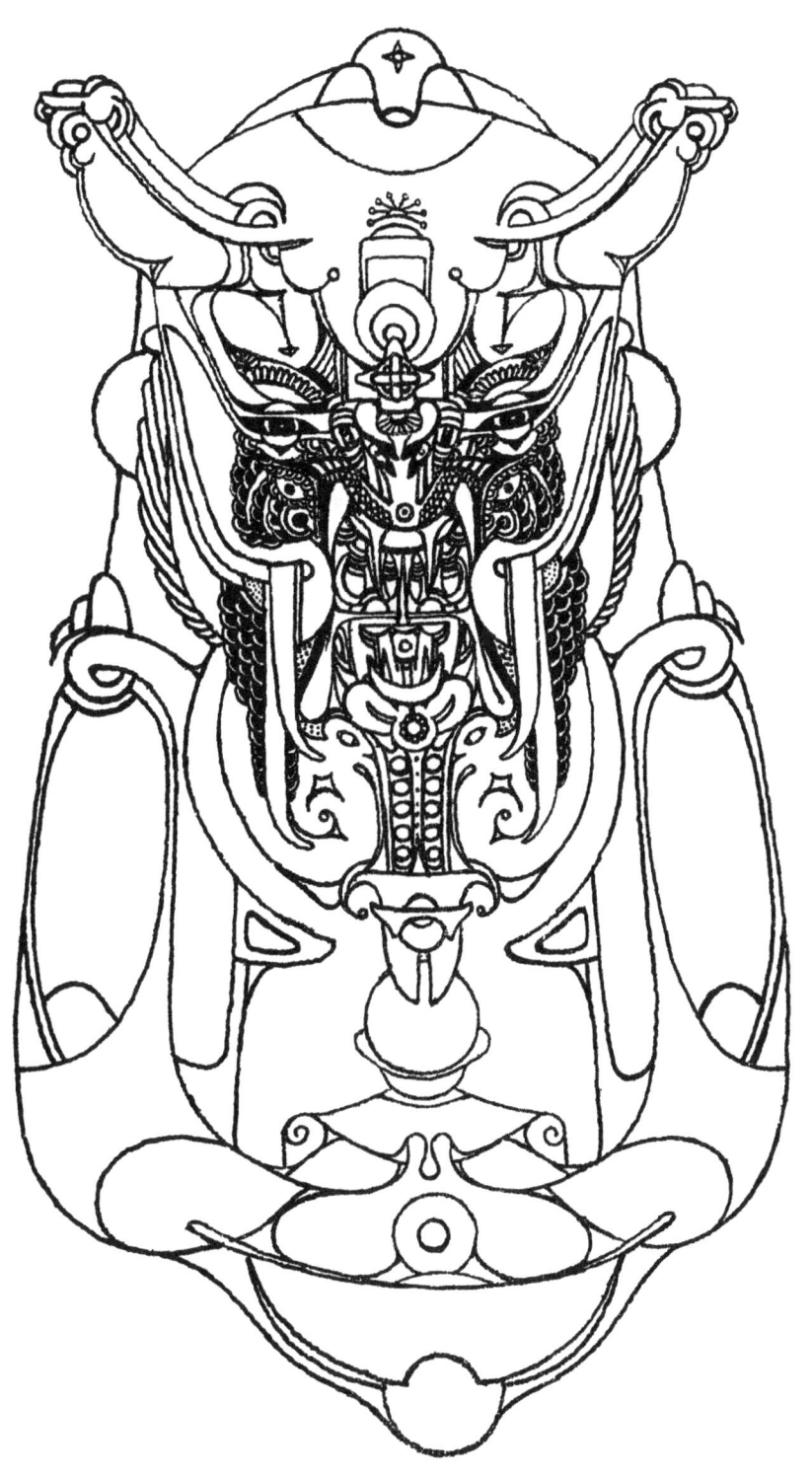

The Passage of the Moon

The Passage of the Moon

This here is the vehicle of the sun, the moon boat on a bank of the interior sea of darkness where the twin rivers of the planets Mars and Venus flow. Here the narrow passage of the Moon is barred by the belt of the six mysterious eggs, from where the six cosmic movements were born, which in turn, will generate gods and men. Here are the approaches of the six passages of the Moon, guarded by an owl-headed dragon with the moon between its horns, loyal to Isis. Here is finally the embryon of the world watched over by two serpents ready to choke it when it will be born, under the vigilant eye of the goddess. From this nocturnal union of the sun and the moon a new heart will arise.

< The Passage of the Moon >

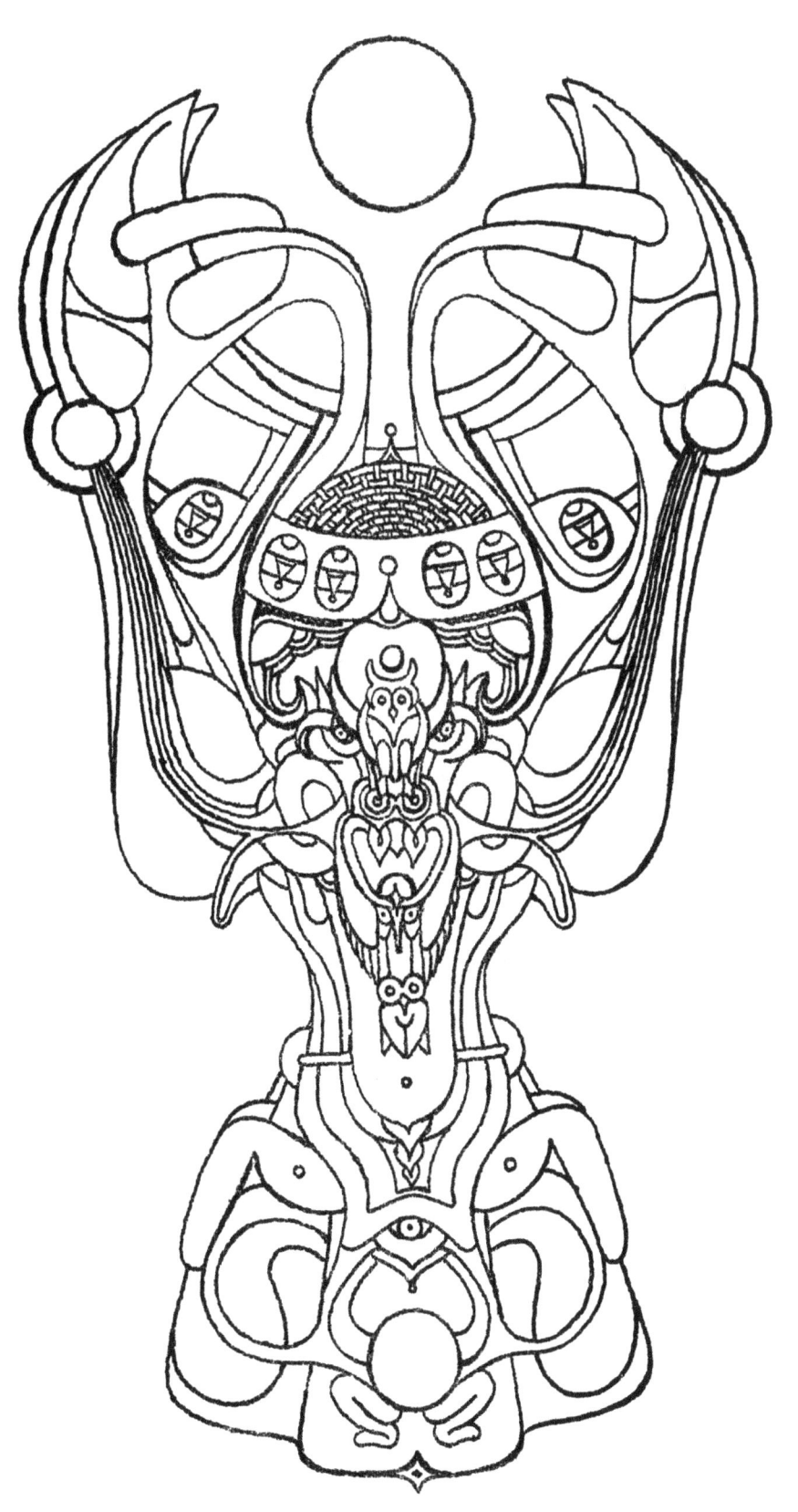

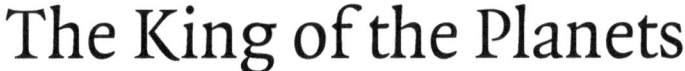

The King of the Planets

The King of the Planets

It's the juggler of the infinite who plays with these nine planets. It is the deer transported by the plumage of the celestial bird. His dress is full of ornaments and of cosmic signs. His feet are satellites and his abdomen encloses again two microscopic suns. "He never moves, although he is faster than thought, for even the gods cannot reach him; he cannot be perceived by the primitive organs of sensation. He immensely surpasses the other fast organs of intelligence. He stays immobile, and during this time after having measured the vastness of space, he establishes the system of the worlds."* "He is a circle and a sphere whose center is everywhere and whose periphery is nowhere."**

*ISHA UPANISHAD
**HERMES TRISMEGISTUS

< The King of the Planets >

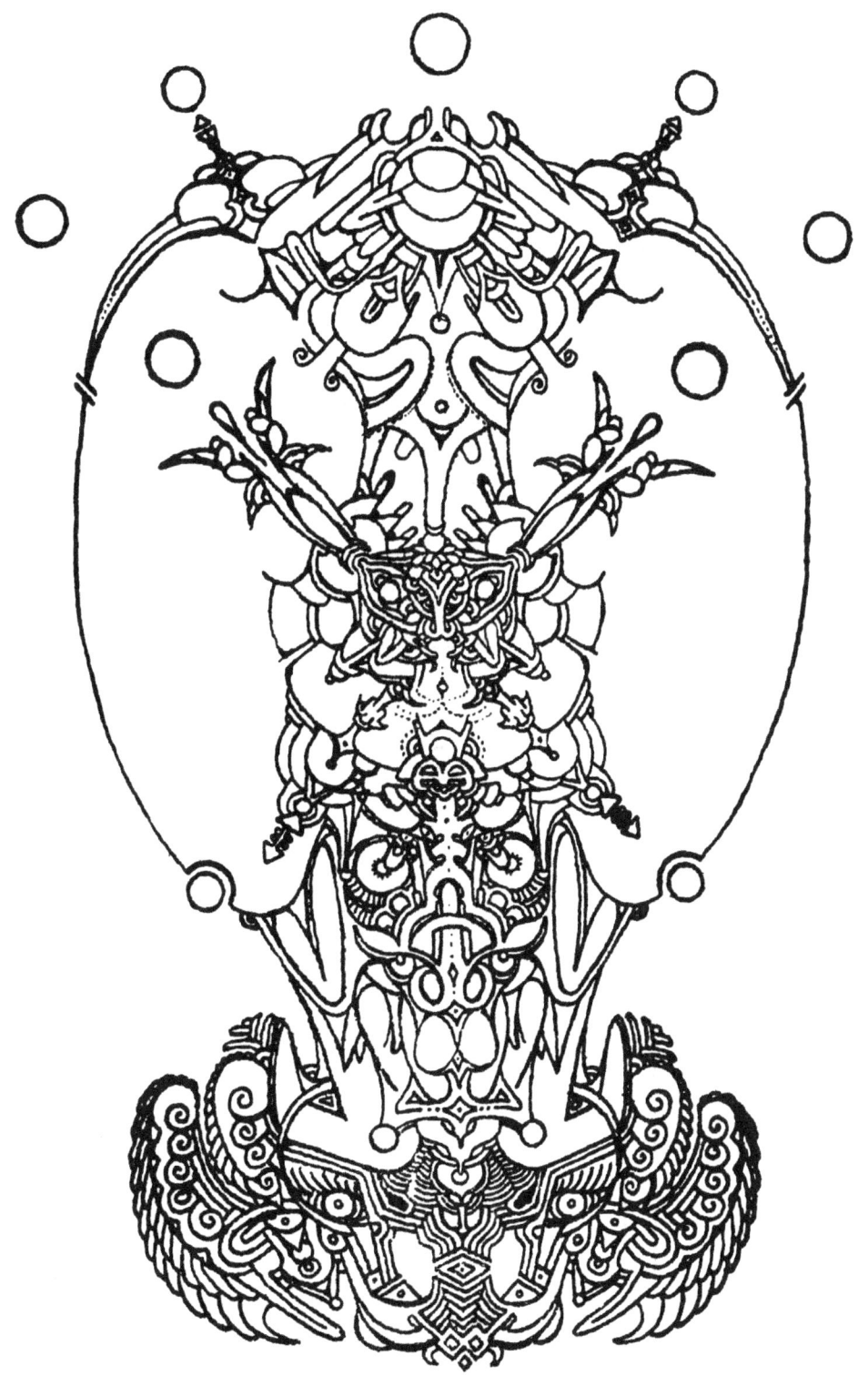

The Genie of Time

The Genie of Time

Responsible for all that grows and perishes, for the creation and the destruction, "HE had the following thought: Here are the worlds. So he took out of the waters and formed a being clothed with a body. He saw it, and of this being, contemplated in this manner, the mouth opened like an egg; from the mouth the word came out; from the word the fire proceeded. The nostrils extended themselves; through the nostrils the breath of respiration passed; by the breath of respiration the air was spread. The eyes opened themselves; from the eyes a luminous ray appeared: from this luminous ray the sun was produced. The ears dilated themselves; from these ears came hearing; from hearing came the regions of space. The skin inflated; from the skin the hair grew; from the hair were produced the grasses and trees. The chest opened itself; from the chest proceeded the spirit, and from the spirit the moon. The navel lit up; from the navel came ingurgitation; from it, came death. The organ of generation appeared; from this organ flowed the reproductive seed, from there the waters draw their origin."* And so will pass in him the breath of the autumn, the shudder of Spring, the melting of snow, the palace of Summer, and the solitude of Winter.

*THE AITAREYA ARANYAKA, BOOK II, CHAPTER IV

< The Genie of Time >

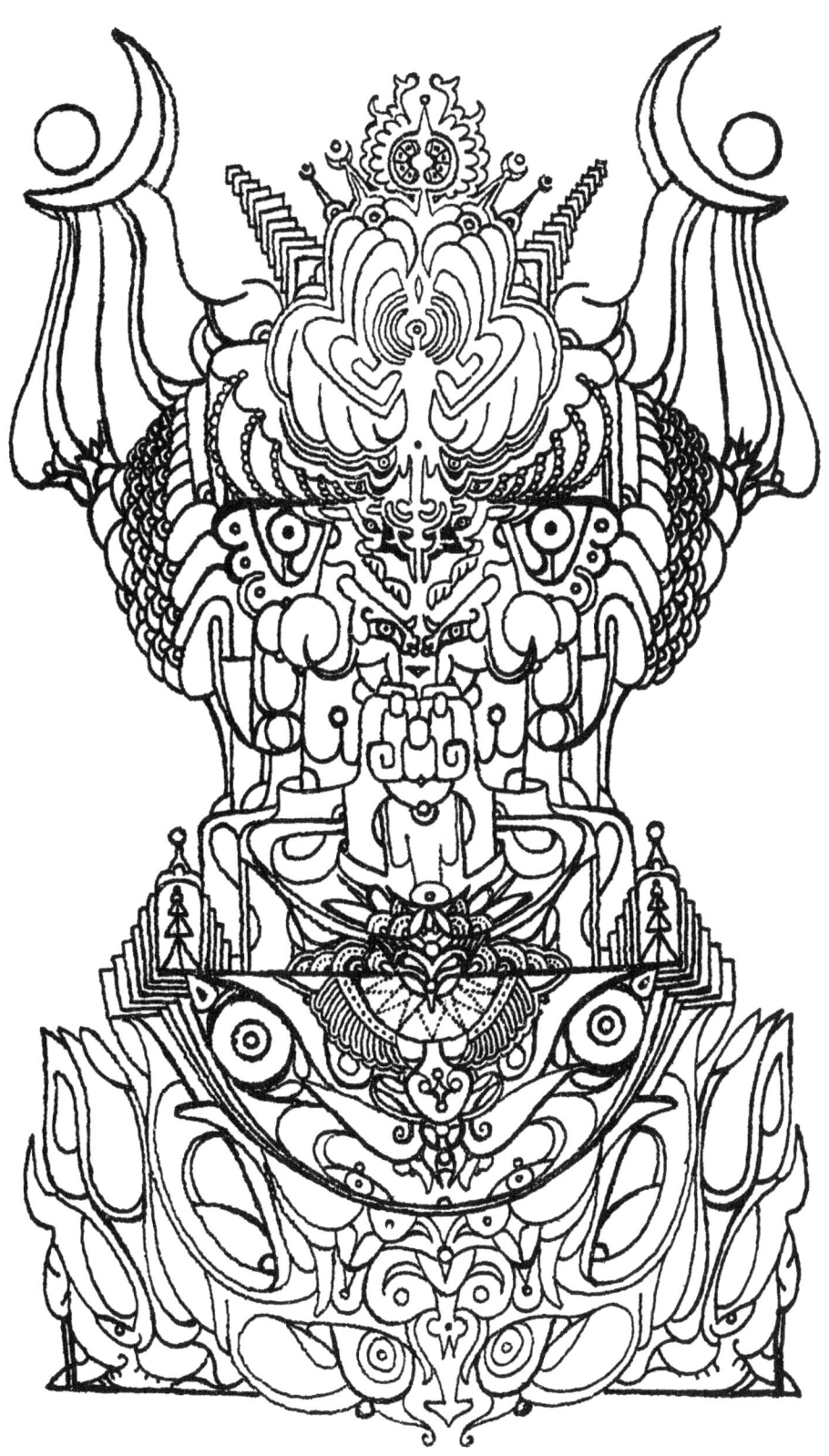

The Tower of Desire

The Tower of Desire

All that attaches us to the world by its attraction and its promise, by way of Chance and the Automaton of the ancient philosophers, is the vision of the revealed tower. It is impossible to erase it; "The face of truth is covered by the veils of thick and prestigious gold. Oh sun nourishing the world... put aside your dazzling rays, hold your shining light that I might contemplate your ravishing form and become part of the divine Being that moves inside you..."* The Tower of Desire, inlaid with planets that grow over it like fruits on a tree, is the beginning, the blossoming and the end of the germinal season, where all the possibilities will finally be realized, reflected, in the prodigious moment when no longer will anything remain to be desired.

*ISHA UPANISHAD

< The Tower of Desire >

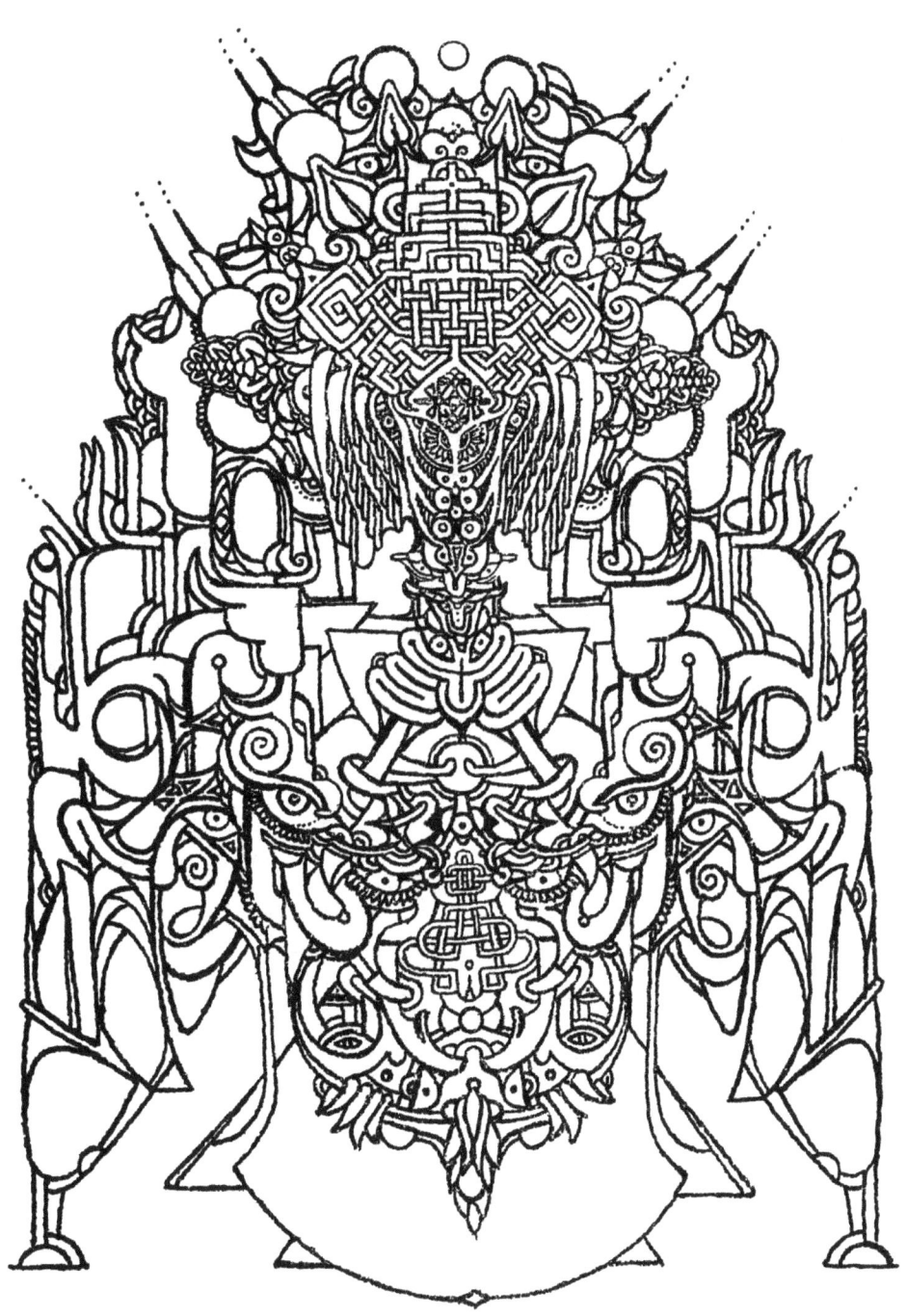

Table of Contents

< Index of Diamond Symbols >

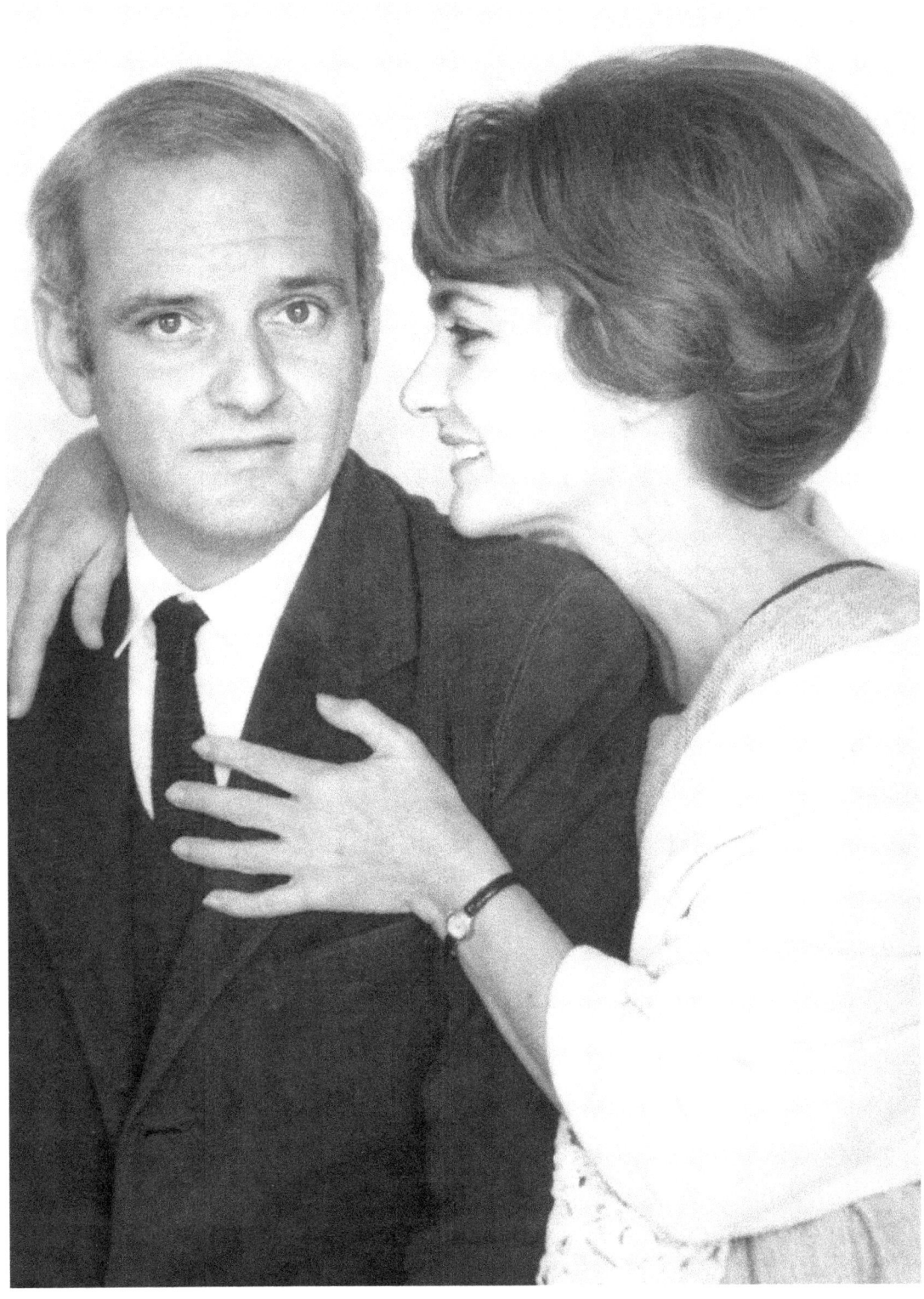

Nanos and Marie, 1960/1961   Photograph by Andreas Embirikos

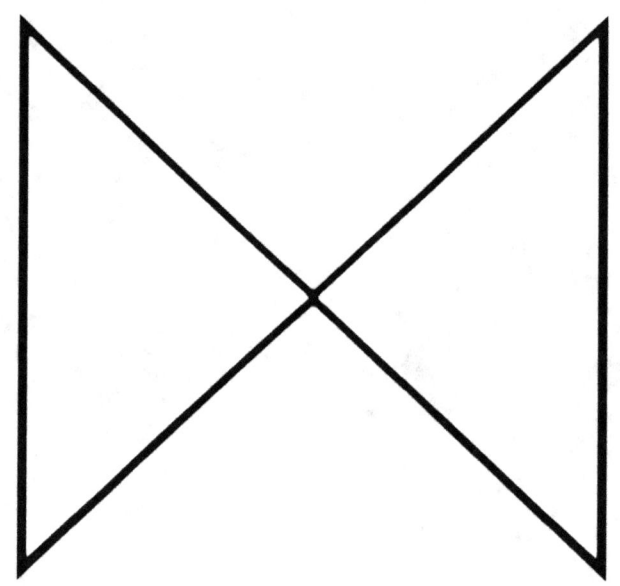

www.ingramcontent.com/pod-product-compliance
Lightning Source LLC
Chambersburg PA
CBHW060008210526

45170CB00017B/2082